# ASYLUM

# Pitt Poetry Series

Ed Ochester, Editor

# ASYLUM

Improvisations on John Clare

## LOLA HASKINS

University of Pittsburgh Press

Published by the University of Pittsburgh Press, Pittsburgh, Pa., 15260
Copyright © 2019, Lola Haskins
All rights reserved
Manufactured in the United States of America
Printed on acid-free paper
10 9 8 7 6 5 4 3 2 1

ISBN 13: 978-0-8229-6580-0
ISBN 10: 0-8229-6580-1

Cover art: Postcard from Denbigh Asylum, 1909.
Cover design: Melissa Dias-Mandoly

# CONTENTS

# THREE

# FOUR

# AUTHOR'S NOTE

The quotes in this book are taken from the diary the poet John Clare kept in 1841, describing his escape from Dr. Matthew Arnold's private insane asylum in Epping Forest and his subsequent struggle to reach his home in Northborough, where he hoped to reunite with Mary, who'd been his childhood sweetheart. He made the eighty-mile journey in four days, sleeping rough and staving off starvation by eating grass, which he said tasted like fresh bread. Six months after this odyssey, Clare was again declared mad and sent to Northampton General Lunatic Asylum where he died twenty-three years later.

I chose this frame for my collection for three reasons: first, because having been solo my entire writing life, I too have often felt like the only soldier in my own army; second, because I thought it relevant that Clare's journal addresses how hard it is to be free; and third, because the fact that "asylum" implies both lunacy and refuge resonates for me. I consider these poems improvisations because I see Clare's changing mental states as matches and my poems as the resulting fires, fires that I hope may, from time to time, burn out of control.

*Having only myself in my army, I led the way.*

# ONE

*To my great luck, I found some trusses of clover piled 6 feet or more squared, which I gladly mounted and slept on. When I awoke, daylight was looking in on every side and fearing my garrison might be taken by storm and myself made prisoner, I left.*

# Mortality

Every thrown stone falls.
But there is a moment first
as it hangs in the air

that the blurred hand
that tossed it will not come again,
thinks the stone as it flies.

# Halfway Down the Block, Your Father

Stops. *It's just congestion,* he says.
*I have congestion,* not naming it—
his lungs as gauzy as a party dress—
explaining instead how the medic
at the VA had told him his heart
was as strong as any fullback's.
We wait while he musters the air for
the next few steps, refusing the car,
with the stubbled pride of an old man
whose frayed shirt collar has been
turned by his dead wife, and, having
no third side, cannot be turned again.

# Bravery Toasts

To hands that have closed around kisses
that might have been bees.

To hips that have ceded control to sex
that snow between parentheses.

To the boy who sees the girl in her tender bones
across the dance floor.

To his heart's small craft, rowing for the horizon
under a gathering sky.

To the motorist rushing towards the heap that
may be a child, as the grass explodes.

To the widow who swore she would
never buy another canary

yet holds its yellow flutter on her finger.

# It

Not-its cross in the air like twilight bats. The slowest counts to ten, her face hidden in her hands. And what when she finishes? Will she part the azaleas one by one, finding only pink wilted trumpets there? Will she crawl under the house, where wasps lie hatching in their paper tunnels? Will she cast door-shaped light into the tool shed? Will she persist until she stalks the cherry bush as her friend holds her breath? Will she lift a step to find her webby sister? Will she creep around the woodpile to spot her brother, curled behind precarious logs? Or will she instead go to her room under the eaves? Does she know what she has? Does she know she can make them hide forever?

# Of Dust on a White Counter

Ava discovers she won't be a kindergartener again.
She collapses to the floor, her head in her hands.

The walker on the beach forgets which way between houses lies home.

The eyes belong to space
but touch is time's, an index finger gathering gray along its length.

# Elegy for Woolah

The dog feels a difference in their caresses.
They circle her, those three who brought her
pigs' ears and rawhide, and threw her sticks.
Her eyes are a lake in the woods, where even
the red leaves have sunk. Her left hind leg has
opened, almost joyously, as if it were saying
*Look, here's bone!* A stranger enters,
slides a needle in, goes. Then they are
four in the room, then three, and
a mound of fur, rising from the steel table
like an island over winter water.

# Marie

Do you know the moment light
goes slant and the trees turn gold?
Have you noticed how it seems
to last longer than other moments?

This is how your life is, when
you're close. Marie's gown is
sprouting tiny flowers but she's
open at the back. *I was dead*

she says. *Am I dead now?*
We tell her no. Then we three
hold hands, and set off like
children as the woods close

around us and softly from
Marie's ceiling it begins to snow.

# On the Way to the Paper Shop

I was almost at the railed plank that crosses
six feet above the beck when I saw a crow
struggling lopsidedly ahead, flapping his wings
as if he couldn't quite remember how they worked.
I stepped back and he safely crossed the bridge
but on the other side he tumbled down the bank
and landed, all bedraggled, in the water. Then
I saw him try to hop onto the nearest root;
over and over I saw him try. He was stubborn
with his life. Finally, I left him there.
Her doctors say my friend Beryl is looking
well. Which is true. But Beryl is no doctor's
fool. She knows what looking means.

*For Beryl Hammill, 1942–2018*

# Down the Hall, a Bell

I can't do it, said the coroner.
I knew this man. Which was
how my father came to lie
on a cold steel table that night
with no one to probe
his nakedness for the gap
through which his life had billowed like a curtain
and then, like the scrim
it was, disappeared.
Down the hall, a bell rings.
We hear it everywhere.

# Serenade

Soon your small yellow leaves
will become meteors

falling through the dark as
each of us will fall

no matter how hard we love,
no matter how close we come

to composing a line the angels
would recite, if only there

were such a perfect line,
if only there were angels.

# When You Live under the Mountain

you do not see the mountain.
What mountain, you ask,
stirring your tea,
as your visitor falls silent
before the clouds.

# The Old Poet

I follow the dark
that spirals

steeply down.
A single star

hangs above me. The night
is glowing

and very cold.

# TWO

*I seemed to pass the milestones very quick in the morning but towards night they seemed to be stretched further asunder.*

# The Interpreters

Only those shallow as creeks in drought misunderstand
our helplessness before landscapes that reach the throat.
The rest of us know that cliffs or clouds can be addressed
only on their own terms, and in languages that have nothing
to do with words. There's a school for this, in a country
which is a long train ride off, and from birth some of us
have aspired to study there. But when our applications are
returned with blank pages inside, we don't know what to do.

So we watch for signs—the tone marks of a hawk's angled
wings before she drops to grass; the directions a dying wave
has fingered onto the sand. We would have despaired long ago
were it not that once in awhile, one of our tongue-tied number
vanishes and returns glorious—fluent in *storm cloud*, *sage*,
or *boiling lava*. A child's aptitude for language may surface
early, as when his mother notices smoke skirling from his mouth,
when she points at the sky, or red rock appearing in his hands
when she says *canyon*. Wanting to keep him close, she may
not tell him about the train. It will not matter. He will find it.

Perhaps there are teachers among us. There's a man I've
been following for hours, who walks the narrow trail as if
he had no feet. I think by that, and by the way his hair
brightens at the base of his neck, he may know. I gather
my pace to see if it was he singing overhead, but
he must have been speaking *sky*, because when I turn
the corner, a cloud is rising off the stones, rimmed
with an eloquence I have encountered only in dreams.

# In Tide Pools

lavender-spined urchins reside. And anemones with wavy mouths. And periwinkle snails, full of themselves because they have been given such a beautiful name. And over these low-dwellers, fine-haired grasses drift as if underwater there were always a wind. And since these communities, not touching, are like language groups that have grown apart, it is not surprising that each has its legends. In one, it is said that the Maker, taking pity on the rocks' empty cups, filled them. In this way, the rocks, once beggars, became kings. In another, that certain stars, unhappy to be among multitudes, found solace in these smaller skies. Elsewhere, it is said that long ago the dwellers in these valleys lived deep. But slowly and slowly, wave-rush drew them upward. And now they are visited every day by her who, breaking over them, leaves parts of herself, which they drink and want for nothing. It is not only humans who have religion. On the edge of the ocean, the finger limpets see the Almighty, and cling.

# In the Stark Lands

there are no trees to slow the wind.
Creatures underground come out only
with the stars. There are no other lights.
The distance to the horizon is a fierce
happiness. This is a portrait of my heart.

# Two for Django

## Trajectory

When you were three,
you jumped off the front porch,
your arms spread.

All these years and you have
not yet become a bird.

\*

## Constellations in the City

The stars could not follow you here, my son.
Still, you look up night after night for home.

# Almost an Island

## Three Poems Written in Pencil on Hotel Notepaper

### Turquoise

The sky loved the bay so much
he melted into her.
Beside such devotion we,
with all our pride, are less than ants.

*

### Ocean Drive, Miami

The hotel fronts pretend to be cake.
Look out!
Los niños are banging their spoons on the table.

*

### A Generation

The piece of paper we were given is too small.
Yet up and down the rows
we bend our heads to the page
and silence falls, as along a street
where slowly, one by one,
the house lights are going out.

# Thirteen Music Boxes

## Luckily, Beauty

Far over my head, an eagle crosses
the dappled light and vanishes.
No cry, no wingbeat, yet I looked up.

\*

## Of Kindness

A sweetgum leans out from its roots
on the hill, to touch
my window when it rains.

\*

## Purple and White

The glories of the morning are
climbing an oak. How often
have I passed them, unawares?

\*

## Fickle

The autumn leaves cling to
each other in their drifts. The
wind has abandoned them all.

\*

**Meditation**

A swirl of bark said: If the tides
inside you lose their way,
what will you have to follow?

\*

**Mantra**

An albino frog squats on a philodendron.
He is white he is waves he sings ragas
while we sleep he is one one one.

\*

**New**

A storm births pink mushrooms.
A doe licks the blood off
her fawn. Whose child is wind?

\*

## A Loss

Across the lake the
leafless trees
have turned to smoke.

\*

## Airboat

The styrofoam cup tossed
over the rail
carries a bitter tang.

\*

## Post-Traumatic

Half buried in the sand
a printer still in its case, intact
but mute forever.

*

## Perseid

An eyebrow of light trailing a red cloud
hisses out in the dark sky waters
on which still float a million stars.

*

## A Table on the Shore

A tenantless shell, rinsed, makes
a spoon
for the delicate soup of the sea.

*

## Amphitrite's Necklace

On the high tide curve, large, slick
beads glittering with sand
from whose past   a mist rises.

## Reflections

The trees in the water tremble at the
slightest wind, the way I shiver not at
his touch but at the thought of his touch.

\*

In a storm, a branch dense as stone
may crash from an oak into
its own image, and pierce it utterly.

\*

Old men's eyebrows skimming
the surface, fly also over
themselves, upside down.

\*

When night falls, the stars
fall into the water. Sitting on
the bank, we stir them with our toes

## Lotuses

On a bend filling in with floating green
small yellow fists are turning to cups.

Beyond them, the dark red river widens.
The river does not know where it is going.

The lotuses open for no other reason than
that they have been persuaded by the sun.

Behind my lids a red light glows.
The air's a hum where the river flows.

# The Oklawaha Is a Braided River

Because what its flow leaves behind has formed islands

*silt, soil fallen from the banks, rising brush and trees*

Because, it is said, myriad channels split off and rejoin it

*I have reached dead ends where galaxies of algae drift*

the mileage from the dam's flush to the St. Johns may
be twelve or fifty-two or any number in between

*and I dream Like river flowers that have no roots*
*in earth, I skirt islands that perpetually make and*
*remake themselves, slip in and out of channels*
*until I'm lost in passages that can't be willed:*
*dark narrows, silver widths, breath.*

## Oklawaha, Divided

Between here and the Silver Run lie acres of trees
drowned for the sakes of men and women who fish
not for food but for trophies, who don't see the point

of anything that can't be hung gape-mouthed from
a hook. Under this bland reach were dozens of
green-and-russet curves lined with laurel oak

and palm, and cypresses at whose feet spider lilies
shone like stars. Here below the dam, water
thunders into the river whose body it spread. This

is the roar of the beast called money and it believes
it will always win. But not yet, for soon enough
its fury is replaced by a pair of late owls seeking

each other through the trees—call and throb,
call and throb, until one takes flight.
Rhythmically across the tangled banks a kingfisher

rises then dips, and vanishes into cypress and
switchcane. We pass a thickly vined arch and this
is how I would like to be married—like a nun,

to take this river, understanding that its water will
always fall through my cupped fingers. A Great Blue
stands sentry in the spatterdock. It should never

have let me me pass, nor the two men casting from
their jon boat with the radio turned up. What kind
of bird do they think they are? Twelve thousand

years ago, our elders hunted these shores. We paddle
by one of their mounds where looters with lanterns
picked through the dirt, looking for something to sell.

Perhaps when the night is full, the bones
they missed slide into the river, to spear what
the moon reveals, swimming over white sand.

We can't see under us any more, but there are
still people who remember when this water
ran as transparent as if it were not there,

good people raised in these woods, who lived
by poaching, who knew how to blind the boats
of the law that came in chase. A cooter slips

off an algaed log. There are only a few today
but come summer, they will line up again
large to small, to plop into the dark, as

they should, at the sound of one of us. Now,
slowly, the river widens. It is dreaming of
the St. Johns, magnificent to it as the sea.

But not yet, we tell it, don't end yet, as on
our left ibis after ibis lifts away until there
are eight, flying in formation. Two meanders

and there are twenty. One more, and I feel
what I felt when I was a child and turned
a page full of print and suddenly there

they were: antelopes, thousands of them
spread across an African plain, for now
flocks of ibis swirl into the air and settle

on a single oak whose branches spread
to receive then. It's a celebration!
It makes everyone in the sky so happy

they confetti their poems and drop them
out their windows without a thought!
But soon, as moments will, this one

passes and we join the wide St. Johns,
where fish camps and houses gleam in the sun.
Someday we will follow it north to a place

we cannot see across. But not today.
Today, we have to face again what we
drowned so people who take reservoirs

for nature can pull their trophies and go
home, people who, if they happen to pass
the mucky water above the dam, will not see

the connection. But it's there: a moth in Brazil,
a clutch of gator eggs in tangled grass, we
who claim to love freedom but fold our hands.

# THREE

*I then suddenly forgot which was north or south and though I narrowly examined both ways I could see no tree or bush or stone heap that I could recollect having passed, so I went on mile after mile almost convinced I was going the same way as I came.*

# Useless

When I take the persona of a lover who says he wouldn't mind in the slightest if I were to be social with someone else, my palm suddenly dampens. But that sensation doesn't make me an actor.

Every dancer worth her salt knows where she is in space. I, on the other hand, wonder how I got here. When I try to move, I stumble over a barstool someone has left by the bed.

The painter parses tubes of viridian, carmine, and ultramarine like birds he is about to release. I mix red, blue, and gambouge like a frenzied kindergartener and end up with mud.

I may, however, be a poet. I am merciless enough. Every day I tear limb from limb sheets of paper I know to be completely innocent.

*For Zbgniew Herbert*

# A Warm Day

If the dog were a cloud, he could run through blue pastures and never catch his hair on a fence. He could leap at other clouds and they would not growl or bite. He could retrieve the sun, which would glow in his mouth and light up all his teeth. And how pleased his mistress would be. Good for YOU, Spot, she'd say.

A stone, drowsing in the August heat, dreams he's a television. He tickles and a mechanic from Houston wins thousands, throbs and a doctor follows a white rump into the supply room. Because of him, a driverless car goes ga-ga for the desert. A rock, laughed at for a pebble, grows fabulous muscles. Oh if the stone were a television, what would not be possible!

Meanwhile, the sun wants only to be touched. It wants it so much that its hair has caught fire. It throws itself at anyone, women, men, even a mouse, scampering across a noon field. Finally, it falls in love with the wide green flanks of the sea. Every day it passions her, but is not fulfilled. Soon, water will crawl over the land and we will all be fish, even Spot the dog, his eyeballs shifting skyward under orby lids.

# Furnitures in a Room

## The Bookcase

has been stripped to her white back. She extends her begging bowl, shelf by shelf, into the air. In response, the young woman sets on her shampoos, perfumes. The bookcase is starving. She wants voices that approach her edge and argue for hours. She also wants, when she is tired, a poet to recite for her, something old with a rabbit in it, or barley sheaves. She wants to know that when the song is finished, the child will come and it will live. If she is not given some of this, and soon, the bookcase will die, and there will be nothing left in the room but bottles, fluffing up their hair and simpering in the mirror.

## The Table

How the table longs to stroke the bed's pink dress. How it tortures him to watch her smooth white skin appear as night after night, someone peels her down. Poor ugly servant, he squats by her side, recipient of glasses, of diagrams of planets that appear and are remade, as if the sublimity of his punishment were written on his back.

## The Mirror

is the plain sort. He likes to reflect the white wall before him. He likes to be the first to know who is opening the door. He registers the little changes, a new continent on the carpet, the way dust gathers other dust to itself around the bed's foot, the way one 6 a.m. the lampshade is tilted at a rakish angle as if it had gone off whistling during the night. He never complains of his lot even to himself, never wishes for rococo cupids or tapestries of hunting scenes or portraits of beautiful naked women, majas or otherwise. He is the husband of her dreams, registers lovingly each new curve and sag of her face, bathes her in his broad light as she comes in.

# Variations on "Twinkle, Twinkle, Little Star" or Something Like That

### Where Wolf

Listen, friend. I know what is and isn't a pillow when I see one and I'm not taking a single clo off in this room let alone getting into bed. So give it up.

### Weird Wolf

A Vietnamese lady is leaning intently over your paw, finishing your French nails. Little bits of fur are floating in the footbath.

### We're Wolf

That's us, bad boy, silhouetted on the hill behind your house. Be nice, or else.

### Whar Wolf?

Skulking at the edge of the clearing, hoping the next tenant will be another old one, easy to catch and swallow.

### Word Wolf

n. 1. A truly bad choice of scrabble partner. 2. Someone who, if you say "Mokie and me like to sniff armpits together," leaves long red scratches down your arm. 3. Someone, who on cold mornings is never at a loss for rime.

### Ward Wolf

In the night-lit hospital a sister, black-and-gray hairs sticking through her wimple, clicks in to check on Granny. Check? Well, not exactly, *check*.

## Wart Wolf

The little mound of hair on your arm that you absentmindedly stroke when you're thinking.

## Whirr Wolf

A pest with wings who meets his petite amie at you and they suck your blood through a straw.

# The Art Critic Tours the Exhibit

## Air Conditioning Vent

To the left of the entry, we find a subtle piece, with only the faintest of boundaries separating it from its environment. Notice how it hints of utility, the way Art must bleed into our lives, how its slatted shadows slide across our faces then fade away, how as we pass it, we almost feel a breeze. This is a metaphor for Life.

## Fire Escape

The Work's maker has labeled her piece EXIT in large red letters. But consider: does not red mean "Stop"? How then can we hope to continue, how can we even wake up in the morning with such dissonance screaming in our ears? Where is the coffee? Where, in fact, is hope? Only the Artist has the key, and where is she now?

## Wastebasket

The shape of this masterpiece echoes the circularity of a mother's arms as she holds her child. But the circle is empty, hinting that in our decadent society there are no children, only tiny adults, mesmerized by violence even from the womb. The Work becomes even richer when we realize that it is also a metaphor for pregnancy, the vessel into which the expectant mother has spewed, morning after morning. And note too that if we choose, the Artist is inviting us to fill that void, contributing our plastic cups, the stubbed-out butts that have known our lips, even the tissues into which we have ejected parts of ourselves.

## Museum Guard

We all wear uniforms in life. That has been depicted before. But it was a magnificent touch, and wholly original, how the sculpture can be seen scratching its balls. For, underneath the trappings of civilization, do not all of us dream of peeing against metaphysical fire hydrants? And (how cleverly suggested) do those of us less fortunate not secretly wish we were men and could perform standing up, shooting a clear stream, never dribbling untidily along inconveniently located hairs? Altogether a wonderful piece. So human. And yet, consider the L and the A across the wide blue yonder of the guard's cap. Before such genius, even this critic is tempted to silence. But not, of course, quite.

# Three Prominent People

## 1

A man from Chicago collected documents, not to read them but so he could tell you how old they were and how many he had. The man invited a professor of Medieval History to see his documents. "My collection is so interesting it deserves an exhibit" he said, and the professor agreed. But before the exhibit could be mounted, the man's oldest document emptied the man's bank account and moved to Buenos Aires, the capital of South America.

## 2

She put on a tight black dress and boots. She painted her lips Fatal Apple and her eyebrows Midnight. After that, she practiced tossing her copper hair picturesquely over one shoulder. She knew if she spoke in a husky enough voice and paused long enough in strategic places, women would resent her and men desire her or vice versa, but in either case, no one would notice the poems.

## 3

He deserved to win. Not everyone can sing out of three holes at once, especially not in harmony, and especially not the Star Spangled Banner.

# The Fruit Detective

On the table are traces of orange blood. There is also a straight mark, probably made by some kind of knife. The detective suspects that by now the orange has been sectioned, but there's always hope until you're sure. He takes samples. Valencia. This year's crop. Dum-de-dum-dum.

The detective puts out an APB. Someone with a grudge against fruit. He cruises the orchards. Nothing turns up except a few bruised individuals, probably died of falls.

A week passes. There are front page pictures of the orange. No one has seen it. They try putting up posters around town. Still nothing. The detective's phone rings. *Yes,* he says. And *yes thanks, I'll be right over.* Another orange. This time, they find the peel. It was brutally torn and tossed in a wastebasket. Probably never knew what hit it, says the detective, looking sadly at the remains.

There is a third killing and a fourth. People are keeping their oranges inside. There is fear about that with oranges off the street, the killer may turn to apples or bananas. The detective needs a breakthrough. He gets it. *If you want to know who killed the oranges,* says a muffled voice. *Come to the phone booth at the corner of 4th and Market. Twenty minutes,* it adds.

The detective hurries on his coat. When he gets to the booth, the phone is already ringing. It is the egg. *I did it,* says the egg, and *I'll do it again.* The detective is not surprised. No one but the egg could have been so hard-boiled.

# Robert and Christopher Up in a Tree

Something there is that doesn't love a squirrel.
For squirrels amuse their sharp little teeth by gnawing on siding.
For they insist on stealing food that was never meant for them
      and when I ask
      *did you think you had wings*, they just laugh
      their nasty little squirrel laughs and go on feeding.
For squirrels scrabble up the outside of my house like bratty children
      and check me out through the window.

For I would enjoy blasting a squirrel.
For I'd start with water cannon, and if that didn't faze,
      tear gas.
For after that, I'd send a warning shot over its furry little tail
      and apres ça,
      le squirrel stew.
For squirrels are not cute.
For squirrels have no redeeming social value.
For however much a squirrel bats his beady eyes
      or dangles his little front paws at me,
      I would never, ever, marry one.

# Ste. Françoise des Croissants

When Françoise was small, she would run her index finger across the mound of butter that sat like a pretty hill on the plain of its wire shelf, finish with the tip, then suck at what remained under her nail. As she grew, she put aside such childish assaults on the larder and began instead to smear her bread heavily back and forth until she got bored, after which she'd lick her knife to a shine. In this way, years passed, years in which she acquired breasts and long hair, black as poppy seed. Then, on the morning of her eighteenth birthday, she went into the kitchen with no more thought than wondering whether there were hard rolls for breakfast or they'd eaten them all for dinner, and there, kneeling before her was a long-haired figure in a chef's cap. When she saw the shaft of light falling from her nonexistent window onto his faint blonde moustache, she knew that he had come from God.

*Mademoiselle*, said the apparition, and Françoise's mouth began immediately to water. *Oui?* seeped from her shiny lips. *You love the butter, Mademoiselle? N'est-ce pas?* And again, though she knew that to love butter too much was a sin, *oui* escaped Françoise. *And the bread?* it said from beneath the moustache. *Oui.* By now, Françoise was shivering.

*Eh bien*, said the angel, whose hands were white not because he was a northern angel (though he was), nor because a miraculous light was shining on them (which of course it was) but because of the flour. And then he beckoned to Françoise, who had taken a shaky step towards the door. *Venez ici,* he said, and produced a plump ball of dough from the pocket in his robe. A male and godly heat came from his direction. Françoise fainted. When she woke, her visitor was gone, and in his place she found twelve crescent moons, aglow in the oven's black sky.

# The Love Song of Frances Jane

*after Francis Jammes*

As my hours fold into twisting alleys, I want to choose a sheep to ride, as sheep have pleased me. I take my stick and scour the wide highways. When I find only cement and sooty air, dark as lambs born wrong, I become angry and say oh, donkeys my friends, I am Frances Jane and I am going to heaven.

And I will find moors there, broad as my body when it covers a man. And there will be skies there that are never simply blue, because good and evil will live in them equally. And there will be mosses there, seducing the high hollows in which I will sink to my thighs and feel I am drowning. And there will be tor-tops there, where everything has already been eaten but still the sheep graze and grow fat. And the sheep there will not run from me but allow me to ride them at my will.

I am Frances Jane and I am going to heaven. I will not live any more in this bowl as if I were something floating in soup. I will take only my feet, and my stick because I am half-blind with this life and must tap away. I will climb to where the stone houses fade then break apart in the wind and I will stand at the top, and turn to the four directions and in each, my robe will stream behind me.

Then I will look up at the one sky, in which every flower of the field, every insect that crawled between petals or lifted up the ground, every small hair that craved another, every flat hand raised to hurt, has materialized, and melted into something else. And I'll spin with wide arms. And when the world blends, *I am Frances Jane*, I will say. *Frances Jane*. And the God-wind that never leaves the tops will blow back into my face everything I am and will be to you, as I cover you with my nakedness and look into your eyes.

# Some Reflections on Theatre

*for T. S., after seeing* Arcadia *performed in a Yorkshire little theatre*

The actors are the wood from which an audience's lifeboats are built. If it has not been stacked properly, and for long enough, the passengers' only hope is that if the ship does founder, it will do it close enough to land for them to swim ashore.

Light or its withholding has its consequences. If a play's action takes place in the dark through an error on the technical side, its watchers will think they're on a train that has entered a tunnel under miles of water or that they're all suddenly dead. If there's too much light, even the tenderest moments will hint of torture to come. And when, out in the house, the young man slides an arm around his date's bare shoulders, he will feel a twinge of apprehension, as if his last night's turn with her roommate were about to be played back.

If a wall collapses when an actor slams a door, it will be the difference in the way a man looks at his wife, before and after he has been through the contents of her bureau. It also signifies if the set has taken the watchers to the wrong century, but less, since they may go anyhow into the street with the same fears under their hair as they'd have walked with a hundred years before.

Yet none of this matters even for the instant it takes eyelashes to brush the cheek, if the playwright has not lived among the angels. All over the theatre, ticket stubs in pockets or purses glow or do not glow. And when the tickets are carried home, they will either wilt, or bloom, like paper flowers that open in water, their colors inherent in their construction but unknown until this moment.

# Mistakes

When you play Beethoven, leave the mistakes in. Don't cover them by hurrying ahead as if you had a train to catch or by repeating the phrase, but correctly. You should never lie when you play because playing is like the core of an apple, it is the most passionate place, the most unashamed. It is the place the seeds are scattered from which fill the springtime hills with green.

In drawing, don't erase. Your botched lines are gestures that shiver in the air around the gesture which multiplies until one more touch, and it will throw back its head in ecstasy. Haven't you felt that way in bed at night, sensing your lover's foot an inch from your own?

When you write a poem, the mistakes are not gone. They peer into the window from the back of the page. They have been trying to tell such an important secret that they stammer and stutter, but in the end a few trembly words escape so that their mother, who loves her children whether the secret is beautiful or terrible, sees what they mean.

# Message Received in the Engine Room

Dot

A speck floating on the lake of my eye, neither boon nor menace
yet, but something there . . . let's say in the distant sky this morning
I see an approach.

It could be an old fear, Daddy with his clogged lungs, coughing
closer. Or maybe it's a plane loaded with something hard and bad.
Or maybe it's a gift,

someone has sent me wings. Huge white ones—a surplice—so I
can soar like the ghost of myself, higher, more dangerous, and,
shaken from gravity, more true.

Dot

We are a blink on your map—a packing shed, eight peeling houses,
six trailers, and a convenience store. Since the tornado, we do not
believe we will be spared.

The palms which bled their orange fruit to the road then lay down
then rose to that hot swirl are gone. The twisted pines have been
taken away, the caught child

put into the ground. It was days before our switches worked,
weeks before we did not see air through the mouths our roofs
had become

but we may never again trust silence, the weather that settles
in a room between husband and wife looking like peace,
the slowly yellowing sky.

Dot

A black circle pasted on a cheek, an accent, as if beauty could
be controlled, as if it would not always burst into flame, moles
and freckles igniting a woman's face

to wild falling, like comets, like meteor showers, or no, like
a night blaze against the black hips of hills, against the skeletons
of eaten trees the dry summer

Jack and married Catherine gave in, and from his window on
that curving street with its elms and tract houses, they saw
the whole world burning.

Dash

In the middle of your illness, you ask for help. Tiny glittery
pills appear and you conjure your doctor,
a garden in her flowered dress

as your air returns and you yawn, stretching, the blue
satin sleeve sliding up your arm
and it will always be this easy,

you are living the movie you saw
when you were ten,
and Fred Astaire tap-danced up

a hotel room wall and you can do that too,
you will never die, not you, never, in
the middle of your illness, you.

Dash

On the straight, stay in your lane, this is the race for hares,
no one asks if you can last.

Fast-twitch makes this event, no one in the stand goes for
sandwiches and beer, one hot roar and it's over,

what you trained on mountaintops for, the weeks, the years,
learning to hear your coach when he says nothing

but runs ahead, learning breath by breath, you who were
raised on the flat, what to do with thin air.

Dash

At night the nurses send the doctors away and they let the man
in the raincoat in, she says,

and they go into my bathroom and whisper. She twitches on the bed
as if her hands and feet were tied.

The shunt in her abdomen shifts and a red stain appears on the sheet.
We ring the bell. A bearded nurse arrives and

vanishes. It's planned, says grandmother. They put dashes on
the floor with masking tape and they all walk on that.

Dot

My name slides between the dots into the pale sea until
it is no name at all

and the dots fade to ships impossible to recover as, where
water meets sky they hose by-catch

from their decks, dead silver on the roll, surging towards
shore where children shade their eyes against the sun

which nevertheless violates the space between their lashes,
the way I signed my name to be safe

not to fall into disjunct small fish, now drifting forward,
now surging back.

Dot

A spot on the corner of Harold's lip who thought not much of it
until it bloomed in mauve and palest yellow

for him, for Harold, who had consigned the wait-a-bits to
Florence, who curved more towards the earth

each year, coaxing blossoms from the dirt, a comet of it always
somewhere on her cheek where she had brushed back

a strand of hair, and Florence never thought of this, thought
Harold, as his work deepened from

lip to bone and his mouth flowered as it did in the end,
exotic and glorious from its sweet wormy depths.

Dot

Perhaps to everything there is a last, a last dawn slant of light,
a last gold sherry, the last word

someone's hand will make before the fingers relax. Or not.
Maybe punctuation's fable, the lie a play ends with

so its characters can pick up from there, lifting new scripts,
their parts circled, turning the pages of air.

# FOUR

*Mary was not there, neither could I get any information about her further than the old story of her being dead six years, but I took no notice of the blarney. So here I am, homeless at home, and half-gratified to feel I can be happy anywhere.*

# Altar

Between Rhylstone and Cracoe the plague stone lies, tangled in nettle and fern, where once the villagers in the one that had not sickened left sustenance for their neighbors in the other—turnips and potatoes, tobacco and vinegars, and woolen mantles, cotton shifts dyed with tea, caps, scarves, trousers and skirts for those cold with fever—then crept off home to sit by their firesides from whence, though they found no tokens on their breasts or backs nor risings under their ears or armpits, they swore they could feel in their chests the coughs that poured from the dying like the blood of Christ. And in the mornings while their own babies slept, the pale faces of children— they all saw them—would drift over their roofs like mist off the hills, then vanish as if they had never been.

# The Wig-Dusting Hole

A smooth-finished passage into the inglenook hides, head-
high, behind a carved cover. Lice and other biting creatures
infested wigs in those days, the more vain the man, the
bigger—and more plaguey—the wig he put on his head.
Lice were not, of course, acceptable, so enter cyanide. But
the gentry would rid themselves of both, so a servant would
be sent to grind the poison to powder and spread it thickly
then put a stick inside a wig, and open the dusting hole.
Averting his face, he'd shake his burden until both dead lice
and cyanide flew, or so he was told, into the fire and up the
chimney. No one complained when he sickened. No one
sighed when he vanished.

# An Incident Involving Timothy Crowther,
## Town Clerk of Skipton, 1761

When they asked Crowther where their twenty-days-missing neighbor had gone, he bade them bring him a boy of thirteen, which they did. And when Crowther and the boy were alone, Crowther put him—Jonas—to bed, covered him warmly, and gave him a looking glass. "Whom do you want to see?" asked Crowther to which Jonas answered, because he was afraid, "my mother," and presently she appeared in the glass, dressed as she had been but holding a lock of wool.

Then she vanished, and in her place Jonas saw the missing man, leaning half off his horse, riding to an alehouse, where he downed two pints and changed a guinea to pay, while in the flickering light two further men, a big and a small, watched, then went outside. And when the drunkard crested Windle Hill, they pulled him off his horse, relieved him of his silver, strangled him with his own kerchief, and dangling his body between them, threw it into a pit. The next day Jonas led his neighbors to the place, though he had never before been there.

John Wesley dismissed this tale but the rest of us know that Christ is not the only miracle maker, for we have seen a man who is not Christian draw the animal he intends to kill and thereby kill it—or sing into the mouth of a dying girl and with his song return her breath. And we also know that some of us are born with powers whose effects will be denounced, out of conviction they should not exist or from the jealousy that can seep from anyone's soul, even a priest's, like the dark-brown liquid that wells from bog grass.

# Below High Bradley

I cross a tiny bridge into muddy grass pocked with hoof prints, round a bleating sea of soiled white backs, scale three stiles and enter a walled lane where one by one hooded forms are looming through fog. I step aside, out of respect. When the procession has passed and the lane is mist again, I tuck my basket of bread under one arm, gather up my habit, and walk on. As I start down the scree that leads to the Abbey, love streams over my wimple like rain, and I thank the Lord Jesus, who has given us shoes.

# Destiny

A large painting hangs in the sitting room of my new house. It shows Lady Anne in the entry hall of Skipton Castle, consoling her four year old, who will soon be hidden to keep him safe from the avenging armies of the Red Rose. Behind the two, in dark brown shadow, her hands folded, stands a nurse. Lady Anne's other children are already gone, two to the sea, one to a shepherd's hut. Of the four, three will return but this child, this child will die.

An owl is singing in the woods. Another answers as I finish the last moonlit step and enter the hall. The flags chill my feet inside their thin shoes. Nonny wraps me in her cape and picks me up as if I were a baby. *Mamma, don't let her take me away.*

# Dead Stars

The house had been standing three hundred years, but had been derelict as long as anyone in the village could recall. Finally the family gave in, and shed both its burden and generation upon generation of its history. The new owners, a couple from Manchester, hired Nigel to plaster the mouldering stones and replace the front windows, so cracked and clouded they could no longer see across the moors to Hetton, nestled below.

For weeks the house endured the rings of hammers and creaks of crowbars and the patronizing sweep of trowels across its skin. Then one night, as Nigel and his mate were wiping the grout off the last window in the first front room—tomorrow they'd begin the second—they heard a deep-pitched rumble from the closed-up kitchen, then thud after thud as if the barrels of plaster they'd stored there had toppled and rolled.

They looked at each other across the silence that followed then Nigel unlatched the kitchen door reached left, and clicked the switch. Everywhere, barrels lay scattered. Mud was oozing from some of them as if it had been trying to get out. He could taste the anger in the room, feel its energy in the muscles of his arm.

Before they could leave, someone would have to cut the power in the basement. That night, the two of them did it together then single-filed, each with one hand against the wall, up the dank-smelling slippery steps, then walked through the empty, echoing rooms to a motionless sky, spangled with dead stars.

# Bracken

When the Romans brought bracken to the moors
to bed their cattle, they never imagined that it
would spread under the rocks to throttle the
heather that fed the pheasants they also brought.
In spring we sheep tenders burn it to rhizomes but
every fall its spores creep back. And, like love, they
can kill, not in the moment, when we are young
and silly and besotted, but years later, long after
we have forgotten the many times we, without
noticing, breathed them in.

# The Gamekeeper

We met in the wind above Malham Cove
after I skirted a group of Galloways with
calves because last time I was here

a cow had crushed a walker against
a wall because she'd feared his dog.
The keeper said his job was to kill

the foxes at Penn-y-Ghent and on
four farms on the high moors.
Beside him, his terriers yipped and

snarled from their cage in the bed of
the battered truck he'd just nursed up
the rocks. *Every day t'same* he told me.

Until the morning his best terrier
vanished. He could hear it crying
from a rift between stones, but leaning

over, he could make out nothing but
dark. The next day, a potholing lad swung
out of sight and surfaced with the missing

dog, matted and dirty, but alive.
Then the boy went back down for
the skeletons, a woman and a man.

*Bronze age people*, the keeper said.
*And I'm the one as found 'em.*
They're in Leeds museum now.

And added that he's lived here
all his life and never been on holiday.
*Why should I leave?* he asked,

as I, stroking a grandchild's hair,
have also asked. I looked beyond him
then, out over the tops with their

scattered pavements in whose clefts
plants grow deep and wide and green
that grow nowhere else on earth.

# The Benchmark

carved on the side of a rough stone across whose front
gloved fingers point in opposite directions, is faint and

easily missed: an upward arrow balancing a line on which
you and I might rest and scan the moor to where it ends

which, as with any ocean, is always sky. And if we look
this benchmark up, our map will tell us how far we sit

above the tides of Essex and the cries of gulls and the smell
of the sea but the number will be mythical, suggestive only,

like the roc, because it will not account for how deeply
these things are in us nor for the warmth that has seen us

through the salt nights in which we rose and fell with
the waves, for we two have been here longer than any mark,

these seas are where we swam, millennia before the man
was born who climbed this moor and carved this stone.

# The Night after the Total Eclipse

we wanted to see stars so we drove past the villages with
their closed pubs, past the odd house, past the darkened
farms, past the walled monks' road, past Grassington, and
after miles of dips and rises we turned into a field. But the
moon was so huge, so swollen—like lips after too much
kissing—that it paled the sky, and, looking up, we could not
be sure of anything and should we have been adrift at sea, no
sextant ever made could have saved us.

# Across the Tops

our path runs narrow through heather whose purple sprigs,
being September's, are mixed with brown. A bleak sacramental
wind cleans us for Rhylstone Cross and the miles that may
remain to us under this dark-gray roiling sky whose blue patches
open and close in a blink. May no step we take go unnoticed,
may we mark the whirr and complaint of each flushed grouse,
and may we glory in the cold forever, for it is the cold of the sea,
which is grass and heather and birds and sky, and most of all the
breaking light that gleams, wild and holy, in our eyes.

# The Hedgehog

Yesterday, along a walled track
I came upon a dark-brown brush
just the size of my hand. From
under it poked a narrow snout
which, when it sensed my boot,
pulled back as fast as it could.
I know that rush, that flight.
Real fear, imagined fear, it
makes no never mind. There
is something huddled in us all.

# The Swan

She nests on the towpath
like curled snow.
She lunges and strikes

if you try to pass.
She has drawn blood,
pushed cyclists

into the canal. The Saxon
woman crouches
in her hut as the Scots

marauders pour over
the hill, and hisses
with every bone

in her small body:
touch my children
and I will kill you.

# The Masons

who reached across
a pile of stones

to choose the perfect next
are dead. This wall

is their soul. It advances
up the dark green slope

and vanishes against
the sky. But what

of Kettlesing over the hill?
Descend and see,

says the wall.

# Constellated

When the atoms in my body

return to stars

they will not remember

this five am

out my window,

neither the moor

asleep on the horizon,

nor, across her darkened hips,

the scatters

of bright yellow gorse.

# The End of Our Lives Is at Hand!

Oh that we were all lock-pickers, fetters-bursters,
chimney-climbers! That we all wrenched out iron bars
to make our way into the streets! That we all carried
signs, *Down, Abas, Abajo* with what keeps us slow
and fat and puts us to bed by eight and steals our
dreams so we wake tired no matter how many
revolutions the black hand has made since our hair
first mapped our pillows with lines to nowhere. Oh
that we were all roused rabble, elbow to disheveled
elbow, sporting placards we painted ourselves
in letters raggy as crows. Oh that there were not
one unpeopled inch on any boulevard in town!
Oh that when we went home, freed of charges
never lodged though we had been held all our lives,
we did not forget! See the dust shafting from
the small high window over the room? Feel
the confinements on your wrists and ankles,
your bracelets and pretty chains? I know.
Those are you. Were. Flex your fingers so
they make a church, a steeple, flapping birds.

# ACKNOWLEDGMENTS

The author would like to thank the editors of the following publications where poems from this book have appeared:

*American Journal of Poetry:* "The Wig-Dusting Hole," "Constellated," "The Night After the Total Eclipse," and "On the Way to the Paper Shop"; *Asimov's Science Fiction Magazine:* "Variations on 'Twinkle, Twinkle, Little Star' or Something Like That"; *Barrow Street:* "When You Live Under the Mountain" and "The Masons"; *Carolina Quarterly:* "Bravery Toasts"; *Cave Wall:* "Down the Hall, a Bell"; *Crazyhorse:* "Elegy for Woolah"; *Florida Defenders of the Environment Newsletter:* "Oklawaha, Divided"; *Georgia Review:* "Altar" and "In the Stark Lands"; *Green Mountains Review:* "Ste. Françoise des Croissants," "New," "Amphritite's Necklace," and "The End of Our Lives Is at Hand!"; *Hudson Review:* "The Interpreters" and "In Tide Pools"; *I-70 Review:* "The Gamekeeper" and "Marie"; *Lake Effect:* "Trajectory"; *Lightning Key Review:* "Furnitures in a Room"; *Midwest Quarterly:* "Reflections"; *Penn Review:* "The Old Poet"; *Ploughshares:* "A Warm Day"; *Poultry:* "The Art Critic Tours the Exhibit"; *Prime Number Magazine:* "Of Dust on a White Counter"; *Rattle:* "Mortality," "Halfway Down the Block, your Father," and "Three Prominent People"; *Rhino:* "It" and "The Love Song of Frances Jane"; *Salamander:* "Serenade"; *Stand:* "Some Reflections on Theater"; *South Florida Poetry Review*: "Across the Tops"; *SWIMM* (Supporting Women Writers in Miami) poem-a-day: "Three Poems Written in Pencil on Hotel Notepaper"; and *Valley Voices:* "Lotuses"

"Halfway down the block, your Father" was republished in *Best of Rattle. Rattle* also featured that poem, "Mortality" and "Three Prominent People" in *Rattle Online.*

"Serenade" was featured on *Verse Daily.*

"Message Received in the Engine Room" won second place in a narrative poetry contest run by the Japanese James Joyce Society.

"Across the Tops" was shortlisted for the 2018 Bridport Prize.